PLANES

First published in Canada by Whitecap Books
351 Lynn Avenue, North Vancouver, British Columbia, V7J 2C4

Second Printing, 2000

ISBN 1-55285-068-4

Children's Publisher: Linsay Knight
Series Editor: Marie-Louise Taylor
Managing Editor: Loretta Barnard
Art Directors: Carolyn Hewitson and Vicky Short
Design concept: Stan Lamond
Production Manager: Linda Watchorn

Illustrator: Spike Wademan
Consultant: Eric Waite
Writers: Margaret McPhee and Judith Simpson
Educational Consultant: Tanya Dalgleish
Film separation by Pica Colour Separation Overseas Pte Ltd, Singapore
Printed in Hong Kong by Sing Cheong Printing Co. Ltd.

When you see a word in **bold** type, you'll find its meaning in the Glossary at the back of the book.

INVESTIGATE

PLANES

Consultant **Eric Waite**
Illustrator **Spike Wademan**

CONTENTS

CONTENTS

The heartbeat of the plane

Most planes are powered by piston or jet engines. Piston engines work in much the same way as car engines. Most modern aircraft have jet engines. Jet engines propel planes much more quickly than piston engines can.

HOW A JET ENGINE WORKS

A jet engine sucks in air and squeezes, or compresses it before it enters the combustion chamber. Burning fuel inside the combustion chamber makes the air expand and turn a huge fan called a turbine. The air then rushes out through the exhaust at the rear of the engine. This backward push is called **drag** and it thrusts the plane forward. The spinning **turbine** turns the large-bladed compressor at the front of the engine and helps to keep the cycle of air going. The engine pictured here is from a VSTOL plane, which uses a very short runway or no runway at all. VSTOL stands for Vertical or Short Takeoff and Landing.

The Harrier can hover like a helicopter.

The Harrier can fly up and down, sideways and backwards.

A vertical takeoff uses more fuel than a short takeoff.

LOOK AGAIN!

Angled plates within exhaust outlets can be swivelled to alter the direction of thrust.

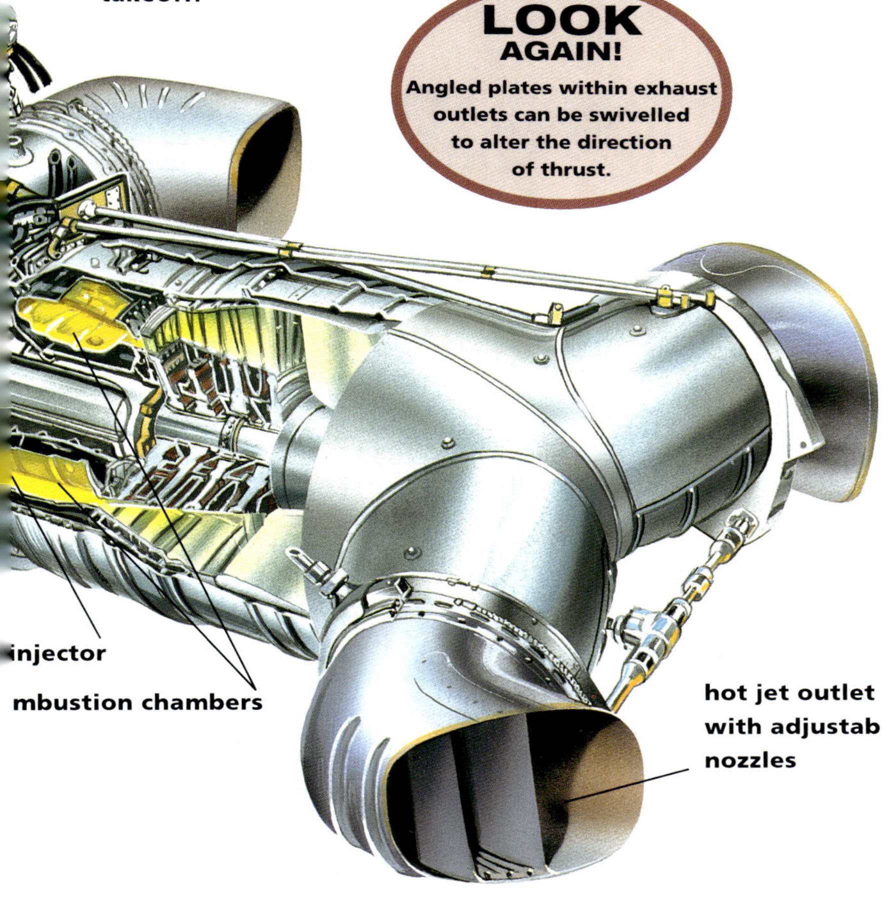

How does flight work?

A plane's wing is more curved on its upper surface than underneath. This special shape is called an ***aerofoil****. The way the air flows around an aerofoil causes an upward force called* ***lift****. This lift, when the plane is in motion, overcomes the weight of the plane and stops gravity pulling it downwards.*

Propeller blades are an aerofoil shape. They are driven by the plane's engine and thrust or propel the aircraft forward as they rotate.

The lines and arrows mark the direction of airflow. They show how air pressure lifts the bird and the plane.

STAYING AIRBORNE

Air has weight, which presses down on everything. When air moves quickly, its pressure, or weight, is lowered. Birds and planes can fly because air behaves in this way. When a bird soars, the air flows faster across the top surfaces of its wings and so has less pressure than the air flowing underneath its wings. The wings lift the whole bird into the low-pressure area above it. A plane's fixed wings work in the same way. Like birds, planes can make three main movements. **Rolling** tilts the plane from side to side. **Pitching** moves the nose up and down. **Yawing** moves the nose left or right.

Moveable parts on wings and tail control rolling, pitching and yawing.

The streamlined shape of birds and planes helps them to move more easily through the air.

A soaring bird looks like a plane. The beak matches the plane's nose and both have tails.

Joseph-Michel and Jacques-Étienne Montgolfier launched a balloon in Annonay, France, in June 1783. They heated the air in the bag by burning straw and wool under the opening in the bottom. At the Palace of Versailles, in front of King Louis XVI, they did it again, this time transporting three startled animals.

LOOK AGAIN!

A duck, a cockerel and a sheep floated aloft for eight minutes on 19 September 1783.

Hot-air balloons usually have containers or baskets hung below them to carry passengers or cargo.

The early days of flying

On 8 August 1709, Bartoloméu de Gusmão, a Brazilian priest and inventor, surprised the court of King John V of Portugal. He sent a small hot-air balloon, made from paper, into the air.

TAKING OFF

Hot air is less dense, or lighter, than cold air. So hot air rises through cold air and floats on it. A balloon is a large airtight bag made of strong, lightweight material. When the air inside is heated, the whole balloon lifts off the ground and floats in the atmosphere. The first flight in a heavier-than-air machine took place in a triplane glider. Inventors discovered that curved wing surfaces give twice the lift of flat ones.

Lawrence Hargrave constructed four large box kites. These lifted him 4.8 metres (16 feet) off the ground at Stanwell Park in New South Wales, Australia, on 12 November 1894. The bi-plane was the direct descendant of Hargrave's box kite.

In 1849 Englishman George Cayley pushed his three-winged glider downhill to help it take off. Inside was a 10-year-old boy. In 1853 Cayley's servant made the first manned glider flight.

Powered flight

The twentieth century began with great advances in flying. In 1901 Alberto Santos-Dumont, a Brazilian living in Paris, set a record for flying in a gasoline-powered airship from Saint-Cloud to the Eiffel Tower and back, a distance of 11 kilometres (7 miles). Then came the Wright brothers.

THE WRIGHT BROTHERS

Orville and Wilbur Wright designed the engine, propeller and body frame for the world's first powered aircraft, which flew at Kitty Hawk in the United States of America in 1903. Charlie Taylor, a mechanic in their bicycle shop, built the engine to their instructions. On 17 December, Orville kept *Flyer I* airborne for 12 seconds on his first flight. It was the Wright brothers who found that the roll, pitch and yaw of a plane must be controlled in flight. They set the basic rules for flight control for all aircraft.

Orville controlled the direction of the plane with his hips, which moved the wing tips.

When Orville pulled the elevator control, the plane rose suddenly into the air.

The rudder at the rear turned the plane from left to right.

Orville Wright wore a peaked cap, a suit, a starched shirt and a tie for his first powered flight.

LOOK AGAIN!

Flyer I **had a small fuel tank under the top wing. The engine turned two propellers.**

Bombs dropped from planes caused fires which destroyed many buildings.

The Sopwith Camel was so-called for the hump that enclosed the breeches which positioned the guns.

Battle in the sky

The Wright brothers and other aviation pioneers hoped that the age of flight would make war impossible. Instead, however, planes became a new weapon in World War I (1914–18). Planes were used to observe battlefields, drop bombs, support ground troops and shoot down enemy aircraft.

DIVING AND DODGING

Fighter planes had to roll and turn quickly. They flew in pairs or in formation and met the enemy at close range. Aerial battles were called dogfights. During World War I, planes had no instruments to help pilots locate attacking aircraft. Pilots had to rely on their own eyes for that. Pilots sneaked up on enemy aircraft from behind. The planes pictured here are a British Sopwith Camel and a German Gotha G. IV bomber.

Inside the Sopwith Camel

The Sopwith Camel was Britain's most successful fighter plane in World War I. The Camel's twin machine-guns—the first twin machine guns in British aircraft—destroyed at least 1,294 enemy planes during World War I.

Cockpits were not closed in with safety glass until the late 1920s. The plane's tiny windscreen gave little protection from the wind and cold.

The pilot held the control column, or 'joystick', between his knees. Moving the joystick made the plane dive or climb or bank from side to side.

LOOK AGAIN!

The pump on the wing strut sent fuel to the engine even when the plane was upside down.

A rudder bar at the pilot's feet allowed him to turn the plane to the right and left.

The infamous Red Baron

Manfred von Richthofen joined Germany's Imperial Air Service in 1915 and began flying as a fighter pilot in September 1916. He commanded a fighter squadron that became known as 'Richthofen's Flying Circus'. All the planes were painted red and von Richthofen was called 'The Red Baron'.

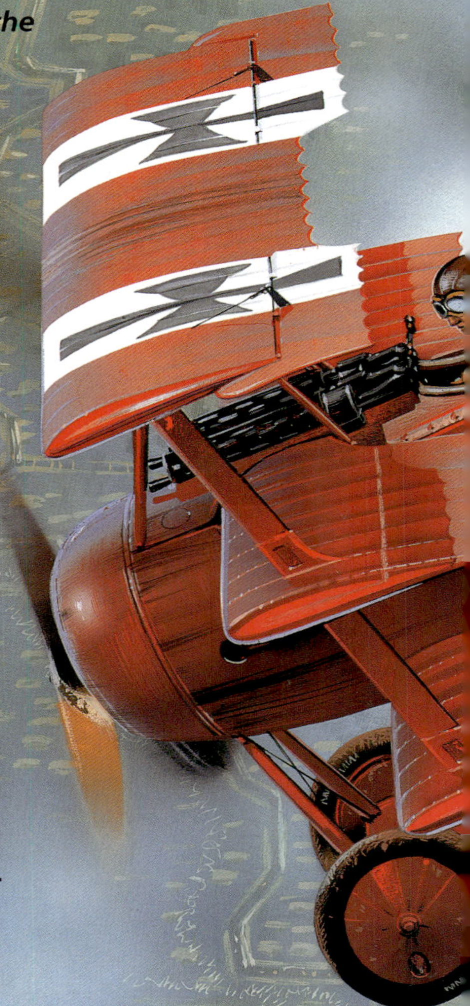

LOOK AGAIN!

A silk scarf stopped the pilot's neck from chafing when he turned to see behind him.

Castor oil, which was used as fuel, sprayed out from the rotary engine. It made both plane and pilot very dirty.

The Red Baron shot down 80 planes in total. He was shot down himself in April 1918.

RICHTHOFEN'S PLANE

Richthofen flew a Fokker triplane designed by Anthony Fokker, a Dutchman. Fokker solved the problem of bullets from forward-mounted guns shooting the propeller to pieces. Before this, it was hard to fire guns without hitting the propeller. In Fokkers, the propeller operated the gun at timed intervals, so the bullets passed through the propeller arc without hitting the blades. A Fokker could dive and turn quickly in the air. In April 1917 Richtofen's squadron shot down 88 British aircraft.

The green plane is a Spad, made by the French, and decorated with tricoloured circles. German planes had Maltese crosses painted on them.

Famous fighters from World War I

The development of flying machines was encouraged during the war. Aircraft designers scrambled to make planes with increased engine power that could carry heavier loads, climb faster and more steeply, and reach higher speeds.

Fuel tanks were located near the engine, so a hit to the plane often resulted in fire.

Bright colouring made the Albatross D.V easy to identify in dogfights.

SHOOTING IT OUT

During the war, engine designers wrestled with the problem of providing more engine power to carry the extra weight of mounted machine guns. Pilots worked out new manoeuvres to position planes with fixed guns. The three aircraft pictured here are biplanes. The German Albatross D.V suffered from structural weaknesses. The British S.E.5 carried a single Vickers gun in the fuselage and a Lewis gun above the wing. Germany's Fokker D.VII became the war's best fighter.

World War I aces

- **Albert Ball** flew S.E.5s in the British Royal Flying Corps. He had 43 victories in air combat before falling victim to enemy gunfire in 1917.
- **Charles Nungesser** was one of France's top aces and finished the war with 45 victories. He died while trying to fly across the Atlantic Ocean in 1927.
- **Edward Vernon Rickenbacker** was World War I's most famous American ace. He achieved 26 victories and wrote a book called *Fighting the Flying Circus*.
- **Ernst Udet** was determined to become a fighter pilot and paid for his own flying lessons. He shot down 62 planes, making him Germany's second highest scoring ace.

FIGHTER PILOTS

Flying fighter planes was very risky. Engine breakdowns caused as many deaths as did enemy bullets. Few airmen carried parachutes. Pilots who shot down five or more enemy aircraft were known as 'aces'. These hits had to be witnessed to count.

With the S.E.5, the British regained the upper hand over the Albatross.

Fokker D.VIIs could loop and roll to escape attacks from behind.

Bombs away!

During World War II (1939–45) improvements were made to engine power, range and speed of aircraft. The new planes were all-metal monoplanes and they played a far greater part in military operations than ever before.* Radar*, a vital means of tracking, was also used extensively during this time.

NIGHT FIGHTING

Here a German Messerschmitt 110 is pursuing a wave of British Lancaster bombers during a night raid. The Messerschmitt was equipped with radar aerials on the nose and with cannon and machine guns. A gunner in the rear of the Messerschmitt could fire straight up into the Lancaster bomber's belly.

Messerschmitt 110s carried a pilot and a rear gunner.

As the war went on, larger bombers were built. Four engines replaced two, so they could fly further distances. Bomb loads became heavier. Lancaster bombers flew in formations, hundreds of planes at a time, to give them the greatest protection from fighter planes. They attacked cities, railway lines, bridges, dams, factories and oil refineries.

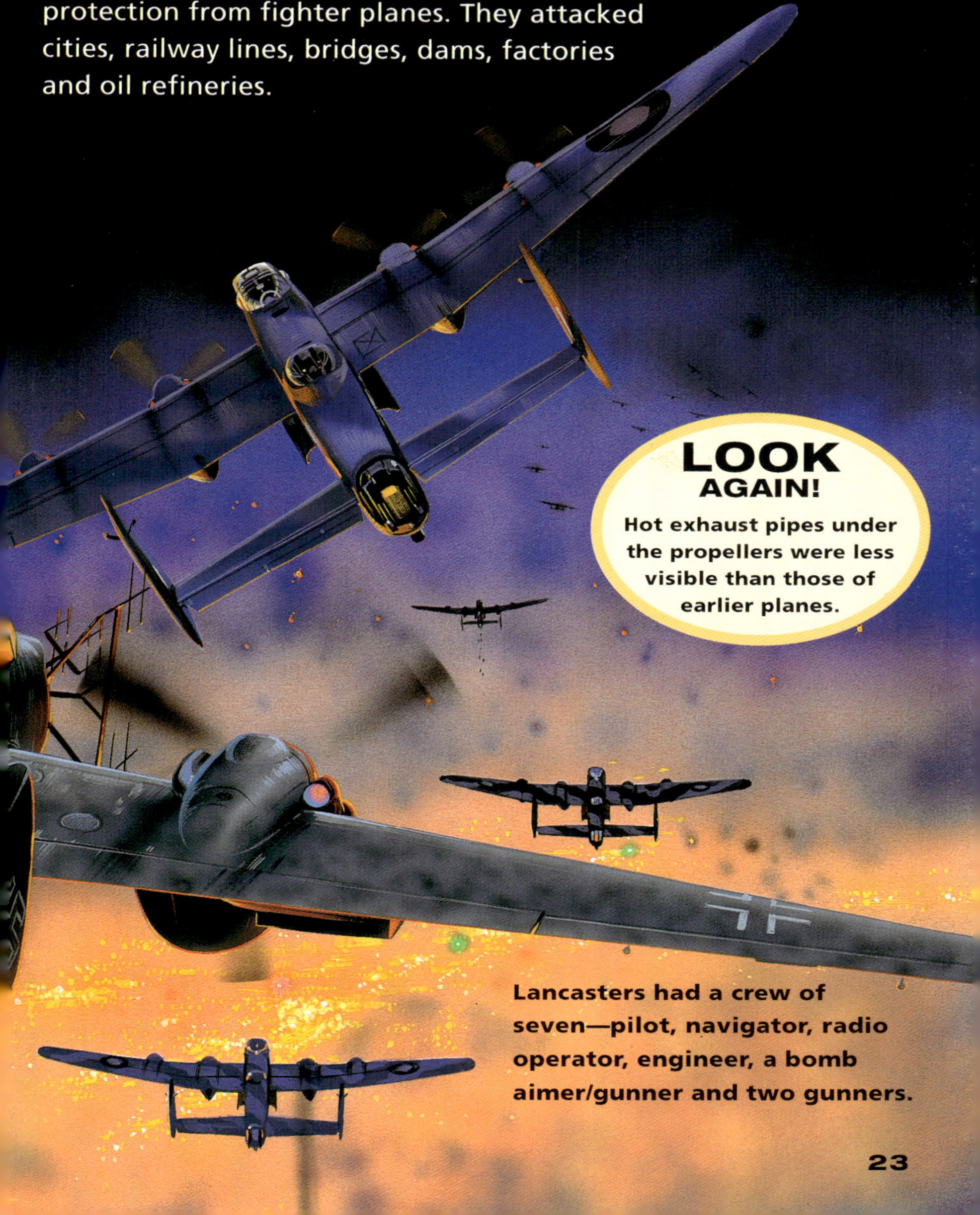

LOOK AGAIN!

Hot exhaust pipes under the propellers were less visible than those of earlier planes.

Lancasters had a crew of seven—pilot, navigator, radio operator, engineer, a bomb aimer/gunner and two gunners.

Carrying the cargo

The need to provide fresh troops and supplies to soldiers fighting on the ground inspired engineers to develop aircraft designed just for transport.

The Horsa Mk II had a hinged nose to allow vehicles to be loaded and unloaded speedily.

LOOK AGAIN!

Soldiers wrote slogans and messages of good luck on the doors of cargo planes.

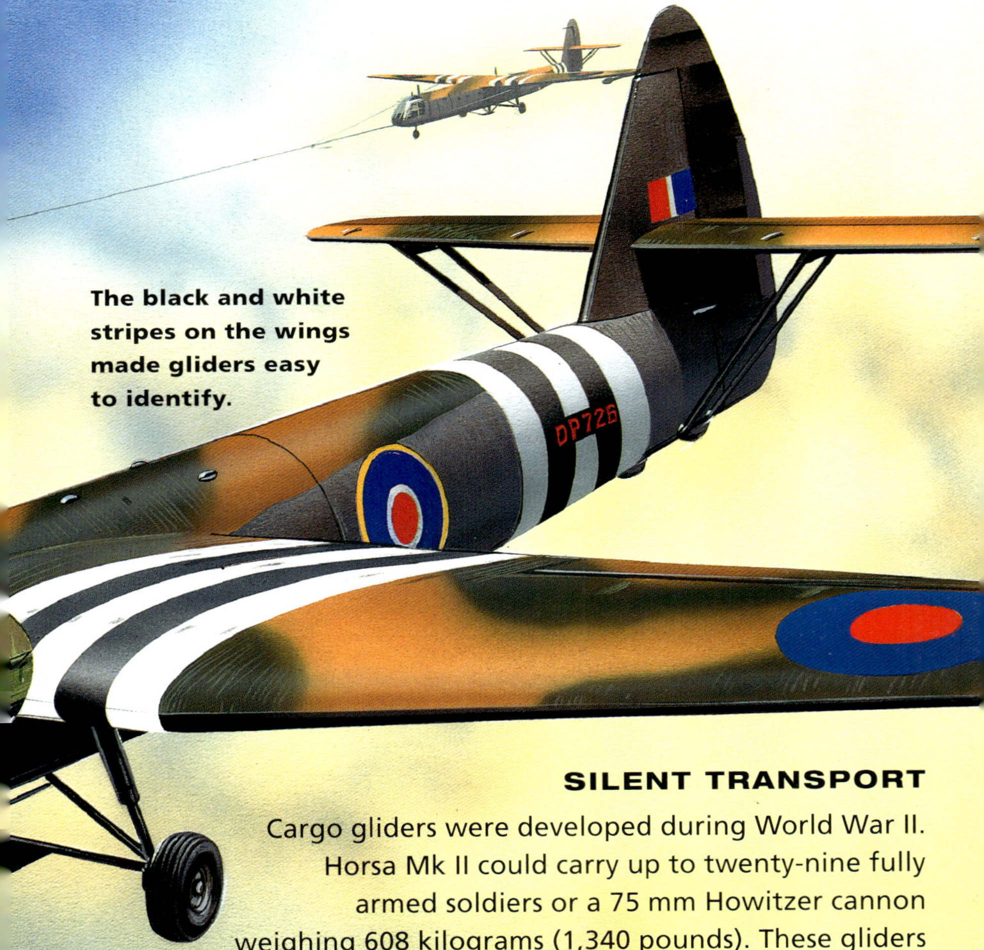

The black and white stripes on the wings made gliders easy to identify.

SILENT TRANSPORT

Cargo gliders were developed during World War II. Horsa Mk II could carry up to twenty-nine fully armed soldiers or a 75 mm Howitzer cannon weighing 608 kilograms (1,340 pounds). These gliders had no engines and were towed into the air by twin- or four-engined planes. Horsa Mk II was towed by the nose. Horsas' large bodies were made of wood and creaked as they glided along at a speed of 160 kilometres (100 miles) per hour. However, when compared with powered planes, they were quiet, and could swoop easily into small fields. Once unloaded, they were abandoned. Both the British and United States armies used Horsas.

Controlling the plane

By World War II, pilots had much more control of the planes they were flying. The single-seater Spitfire was one of Britain's fastest and most famous fighters. In the enclosed cockpit, the pilot faced an array of dials on the instrument panel. The key to these and other features is on the next page.

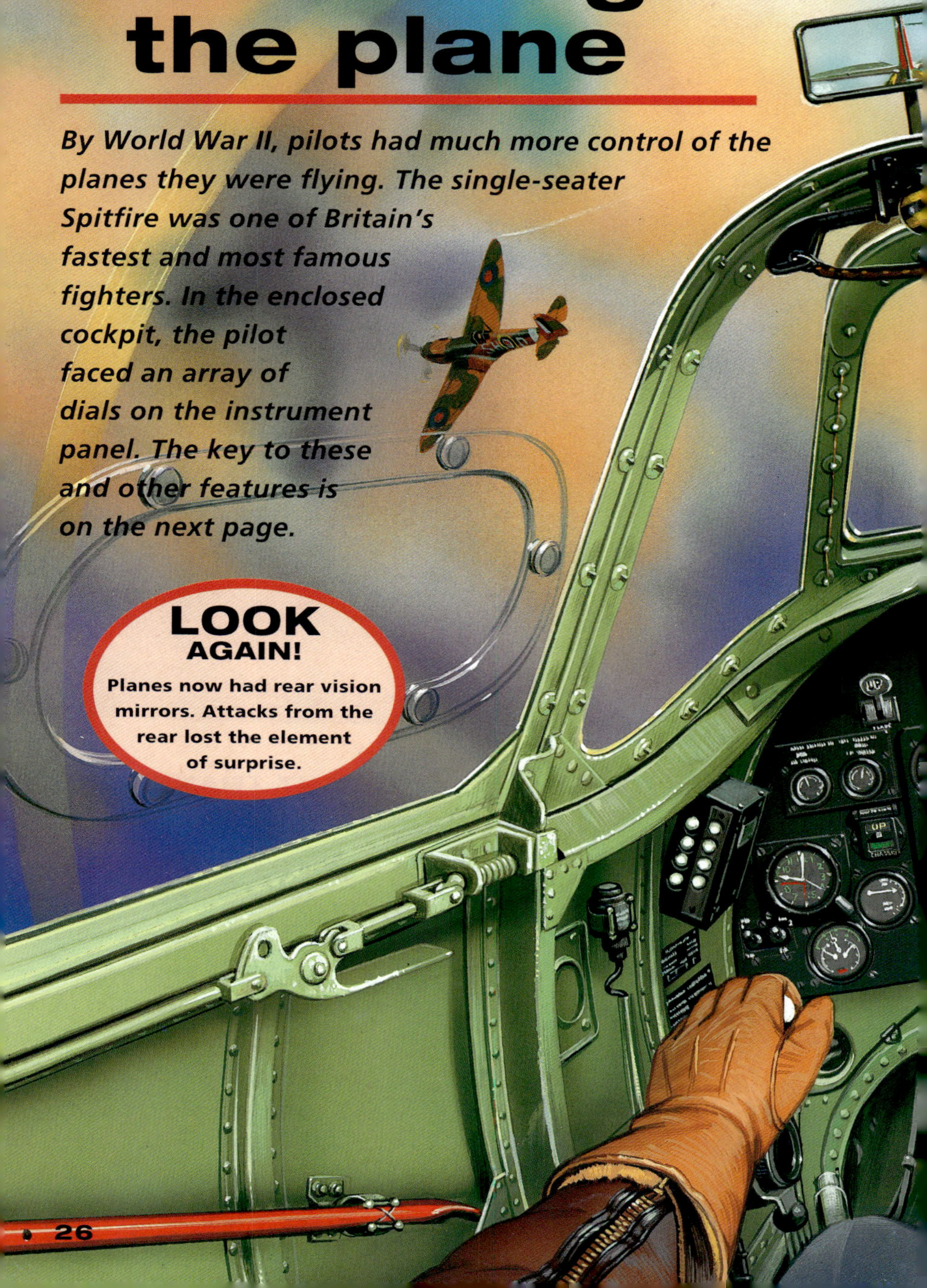

LOOK AGAIN!

Planes now had rear vision mirrors. Attacks from the rear lost the element of surprise.

A bullet-proof windscreen protected the pilot.

Some Spitfires carried bombs for ground attack missions.

Spitfire I was armed with eight machine guns. Later models had cannons as well.

The fighting spitfire

During the Battle of Britain, from August to October 1940, the German Luftwaffe tried to destroy the Royal Air Force in the skies above Britain in preparation for an invasion by sea. Spitfires shot down many German fighter planes.

STREAMLINED FOR SPEED

The Spitfire was one of the first planes to have wheels that could be pulled up out of the airflow. Retractable wheels cut down the drag of the air on the plane's body and increased its speed. The Spitfire's top speed in 1938 was about 580 kilometres (360 miles) per hour.Between 1936 and 1947 more than 20,000 Spitfires were built. The Royal Air Force stopped using them in 1954. About 50 are still airworthy and can still be seen at air shows in Britain, the USA, Australia and New Zealand.

LOOK AGAIN!

The Spitfire pictured was piloted by Alan Deere, a New Zealand ace with 22 confirmed hits.

KEY TO SPITFIRE COCKPIT

1. Ignition switches
2. Pressure gauge
3. Undercarriage indicator
4. Flap lever
5. Breakable escape window
6. Airspeed indicator
7. Gyro compass
8. Reflector gunsight
9. Cockpit opening handle
10. Rear view mirror
11. Engine speed indicator
12. Climb indicator
13. Turn indicator
14. Fuel gauge
15. Joystick
16. Wheels up-and-down operating lever

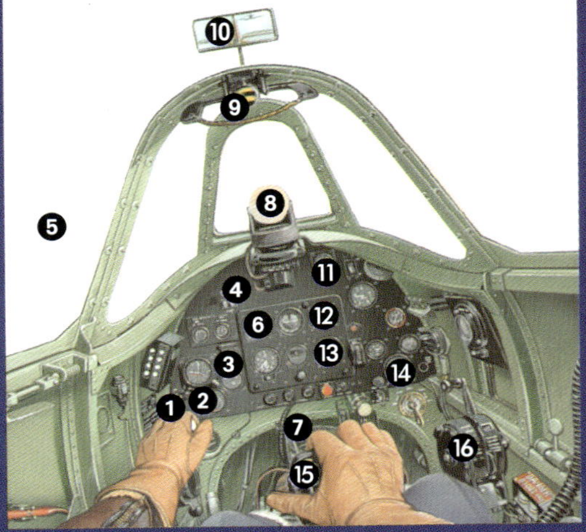

The North American Mustang was able to go further than earlier fighter planes. It could fly at low altitudes and was equipped with rockets.

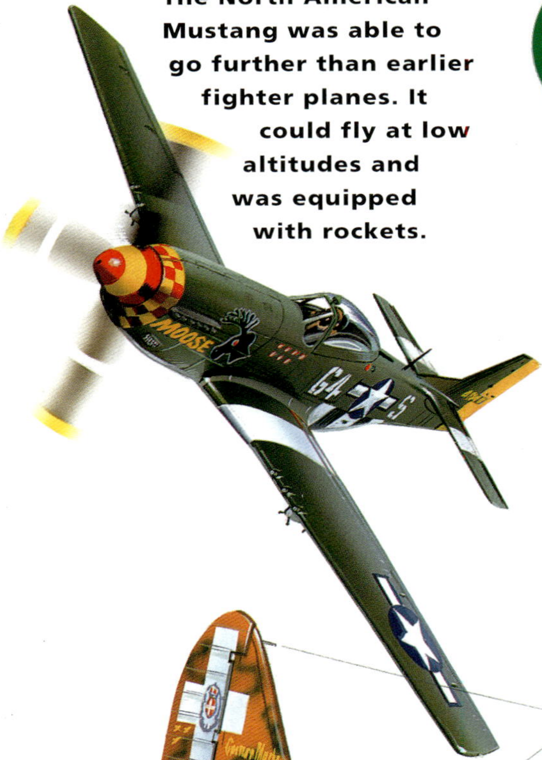

LOOK AGAIN!

Radio transmitter wires outside the planes allowed pilots to contact ground control.

The Japanese Mitsubishi Zero fighter was one of the best performers early in World War II. It was very light and easy to manoeuvre.

The Italian Macchi single-engined fighters flew superbly. These planes were painted in camouflage patterns and decorated with the badges of the flying squadrons.

Flying into battle in World War II

Germany manufactured more aircraft than any other country during World War II. Other countries also making planes included the United States, Britain, France, Italy, Russia, Japan, Australia and Canada. Fighters and bombers powered by jet engines were developed towards the end of the war.

BREATHING EASY

Today all passenger plane cabins are pressurised so that people can breathe air safely and comfortably at high altitudes. However, until the end of World War II, very few planes were pressurised. This meant that fliers had to wear oxygen masks if their planes climbed above 4,267 metres (14,000 feet). Bomber crews often wore them for missions lasting up to 10 hours.

World War II aces

- British pilot **Douglas Bader** lost both legs after an air crash in 1931. He then flew with tin legs. Bader scored 22½ victories.
- **Richard I. Bong** was America's top ace with the American Army Air Force (AAAF). He shot down 40 Japanese planes. Bong was killed in August 1945 testing a jet plane.
- Already an experienced pilot when he joined the German Luftwaffe, **Adolf Galland** ended the war with 104 victories.

Modern warplanes

Modern jet fighters can fly faster, higher and for longer than earlier war planes. They are more manoeuvrable and can carry heavier loads. Most have special radar equipment to locate enemy targets.

Fighter aircraft seldom fly alone. The Tomcat is protecting the A6 Intruder, in the background, allowing the Intruder's pilot to concentrate on the strategic bombing of the bridge.

LOOK AGAIN!

A 'smart bomb' has hit its target—a bridge—without damaging surrounding areas.

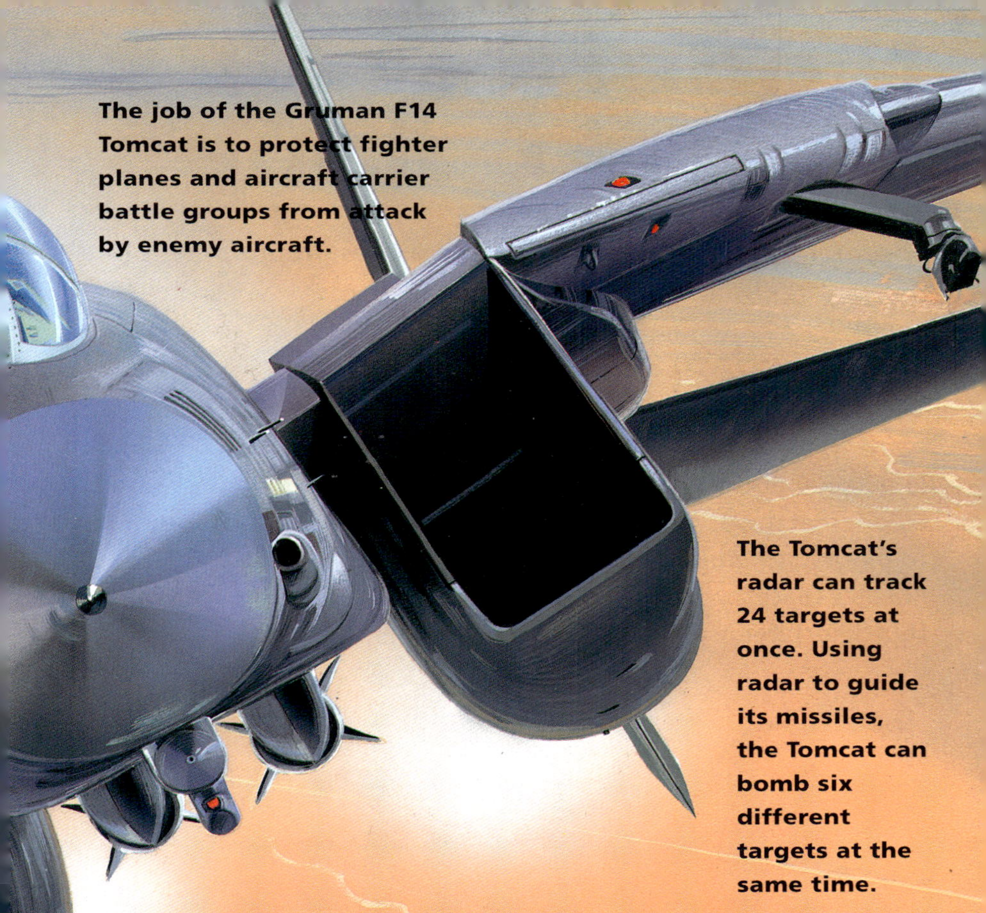

The job of the Gruman F14 Tomcat is to protect fighter planes and aircraft carrier battle groups from attack by enemy aircraft.

The Tomcat's radar can track 24 targets at once. Using radar to guide its missiles, the Tomcat can bomb six different targets at the same time.

SNEAKY PLANES

During World War II fighter bombers came into use in 'strategic bombing'. This is dropping bombs on targets like enemy military bases or bridges and roads. Now, all modern aircraft have radar to help them navigate. By using radar, a bomber can still strike accurately at night or in bad weather. Radar is also used to track enemy planes. Some fighters, called stealth planes, have been designed in ways that make it harder for radar to see them. This means they are not detected by enemy fighters. The Tomcat is a swing-winged aircraft. Their wings are forward for takeoff and landing and back close to the sides of the plane to make them more streamlined when flying.

Modern cargo planes

Enormous cargo planes carry huge pieces of equipment like military tanks and sections of rocket.

WHAT A LOAD!

The massive Russian Antonov An-225 Myria is the biggest cargo plane in the world. It can take off with a load of 453,600 kilograms (1,000,000 pounds), about the same weight as a herd of 60 adult elephants! It was designed for use in the Russian space program, to piggy-back *Buran*, Russia's space shuttle orbiter.

The Lockheed C-5 Galaxy is painted in camouflage patterns to make it harder to see.

The entire nose lifts upwards so cargo can be driven in.

HEAVY WORK

America's Lockheed C-5 Galaxy can also take off with enormous loads. It can carry two M1A1 Abrams tanks or four Sheridan light tanks and five HMMVW four-wheel drive vehicles. Equipment is loaded on ramps lowered from vast doors in the nose and tail.

Military personnel also travel in these cargo planes.

Cargo planes often have to land on short, poorly lit runways. Some can even take off on snow, using skis.

A tank is dropped by parachute from the giant rear doors of a low-flying Hercules cargo plane. This method of delivering cargo is called LAPES, which stands for Low Altitude Parachute Extraction System. It is used when there is no adequate landing strip.

LOOK AGAIN!

When the pilot runs out of room on the knee-pads, notes are written on the side window.

Information is projected onto a see-through screen so the pilot does not need to look down at the instruments. This is called HUD, for head-up display.

The brain of the plane

This is the cockpit of an F/A-18 Hornet, one of the most powerful jet fighters in the world. The key to its features is on the next page.

TAKING NOTES

Before takeoff, the pilot receives instructions from ground control staff. These instructions and other information, such as weather conditions, are often written on the wipe-clean knee-pads which are sewn into the pilot's uniform.

The pilot needs rear view mirrors because the radar shows only what is ahead.

All flying controls are on the throttle and control column.

The Hornet's sting

The 'F' stands for 'fighter' and the 'A' for 'attacker' in the F/A-18 Hornet's name, because this plane is both. It can fight other planes in the air, or attack targets on the ground.

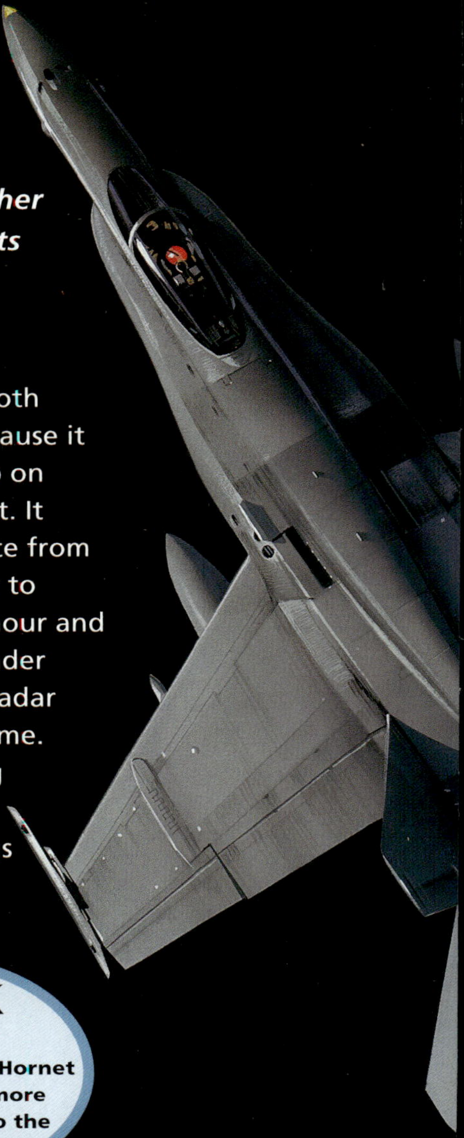

FAST AND FEARSOME

The F/A-18 Hornet operates from both aircraft carriers and land bases. Because it is not a stealth bomber, it shows up on enemy radar, but it is extremely fast. It takes only two minutes to accelerate from 850 kilometres (530 miles) per hour to 1,705 kilometres (1,060 miles) per hour and can fly at Mach 1.8, which is just under twice the speed of sound. Its own radar can track ten targets at the same time. The Hornet has an especially strong undercarriage to withstand catapult launches and hard landings on the deck of an aircraft carrier.

LOOK AGAIN!

The wingtips of the Hornet fold upwards so more planes can fit onto the carrier's deck.

The F/A-18 Hornet is made by McDonnell Douglas. The first F/A-18s began flying in 1982.

KEY TO F/A-18 HORNET COCKPIT

1. Throttle (under left hand)
2. Eject lever
3. Engine status display
4. Master monitor display
5. Up-front control panel
6. Head-up display
7. Rear view mirrors
8. Warning panels
9. Horizontal situation display
10. Multi-function sensor display
11. Weapon release
12. Altitude reference indicator
13. Altimeter and airspeed indicators
14. Standby magnetic compass
15. Radar warning display
16. Altitude indicator
17. Caution light panel
18. Standby eject lever

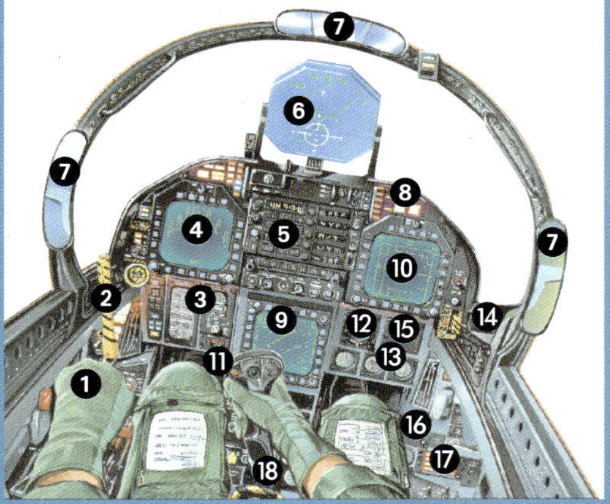

New-age fighters

Modern military aircraft have powerful engines, computer-operated controls, missiles that can follow a target and many ways of seeking out enemy aircraft. They also have tricks to avoid being found.

VANISHING TRICKS

Helicopters are very useful in war. They can take off and land without a runway and can remain hovering in one place in the air. Helicopters with rockets and guns are used to attack tanks and troops. By hiding behind trees, hills and buildings, helicopters can fly very close to the ground, out of the range of radar. Stealth fighter planes trick radar by having many flat surfaces so the radar bounces off in all directions, sending back a confusing message.
Some fighters are painted with radar-absorbing material.

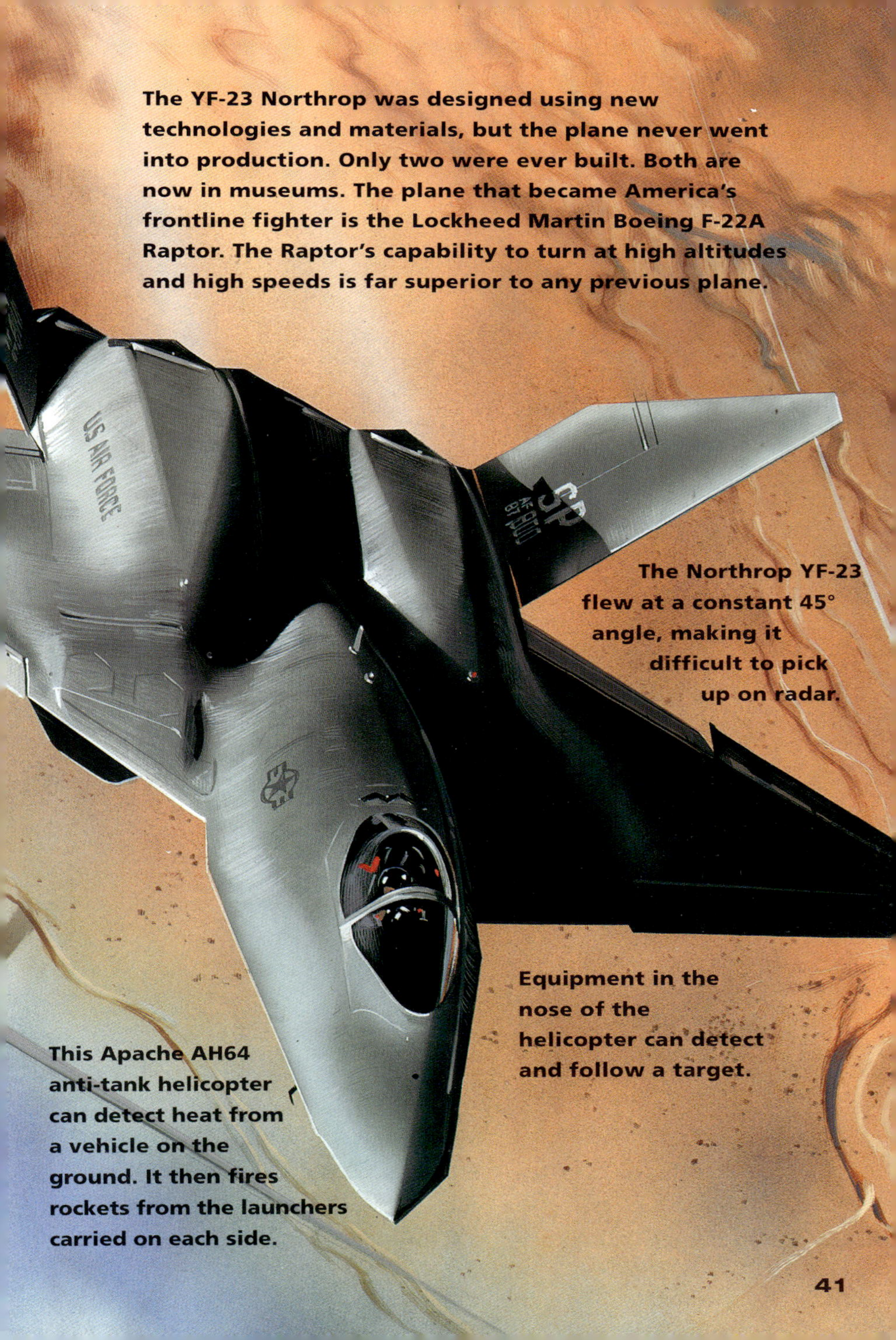

The YF-23 Northrop was designed using new technologies and materials, but the plane never went into production. Only two were ever built. Both are now in museums. The plane that became America's frontline fighter is the Lockheed Martin Boeing F-22A Raptor. The Raptor's capability to turn at high altitudes and high speeds is far superior to any previous plane.

The Northrop YF-23 flew at a constant 45° angle, making it difficult to pick up on radar.

Equipment in the nose of the helicopter can detect and follow a target.

This Apache AH64 anti-tank helicopter can detect heat from a vehicle on the ground. It then fires rockets from the launchers carried on each side.

Tricky landings

An aircraft carrier is a very exciting and noisy place to be. Planes roar into the air. Returning jets slam back on the deck. If they do not hook an arresting wire, they roar off again.

The huge size of the aircraft carrier's deck, about as big as three football fields, makes even the planes seem small.

Arrestor wires can bring a plane travelling at high speeds to a stop very quickly.

FLOATING AERODROME

The back part of the deck, pictured here, has four arrestor wires used for landings. The front part is used for takeoffs. Four giant catapults are located at different angles so planes can take off and land only seconds apart.

HITTING THE DECK

To land, the pilot swoops right down to the deck at high speed, guided by a system of lights. A tailhook dangles from under the plane. Sometimes the hook bangs along the steel deck, sending up a shower of sparks. If the hook catches one of the four strong arrestor wires stretched across the deck, the plane is pulled to a sudden stop. If the hook doesn't catch, the pilot applies full power and climbs away for a second try.

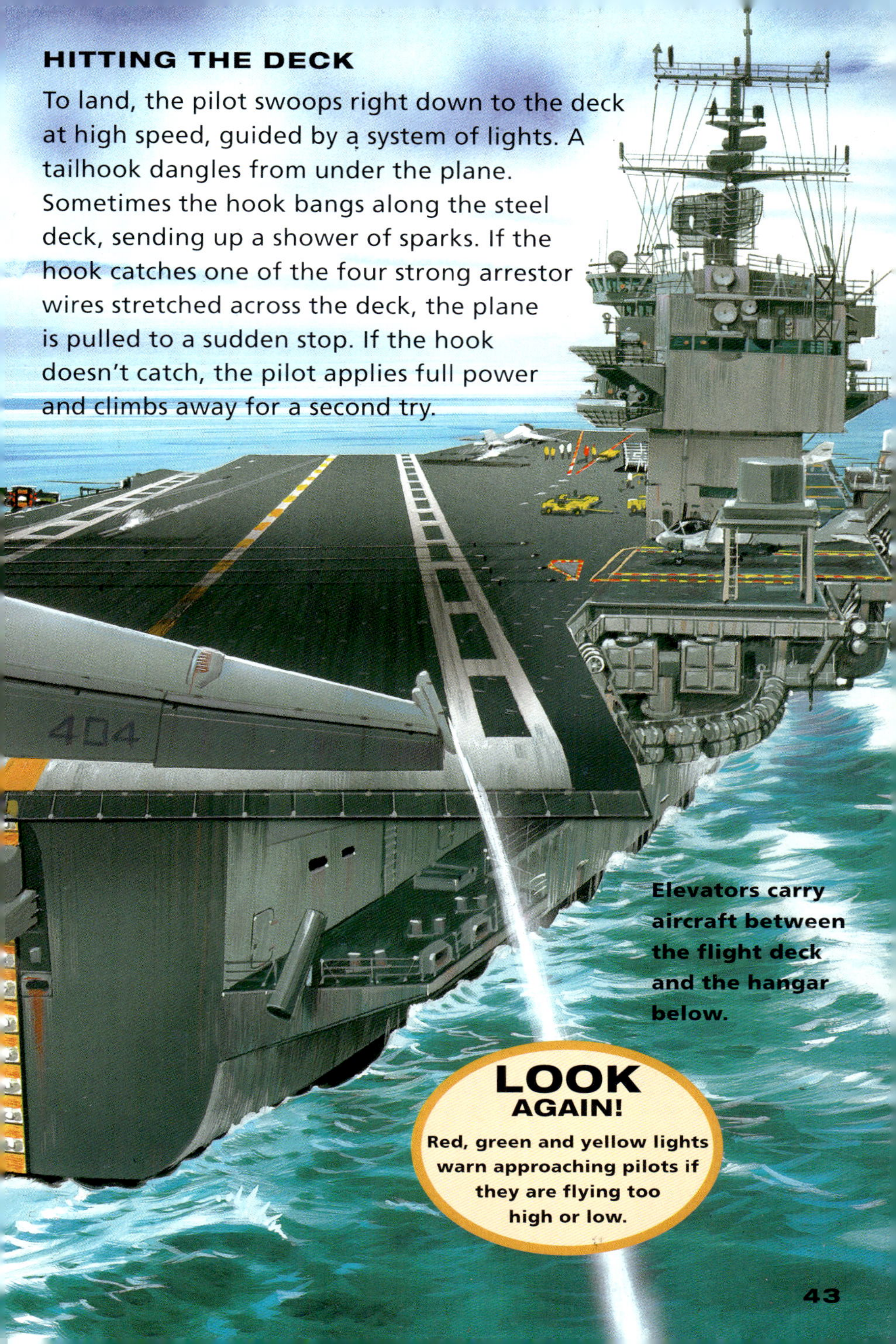

Elevators carry aircraft between the flight deck and the hangar below.

LOOK AGAIN!

Red, green and yellow lights warn approaching pilots if they are flying too high or low.

LOOK AGAIN!

In the DC-3, baggage is stacked piece by piece. In the Concorde it is loaded on trolleys.

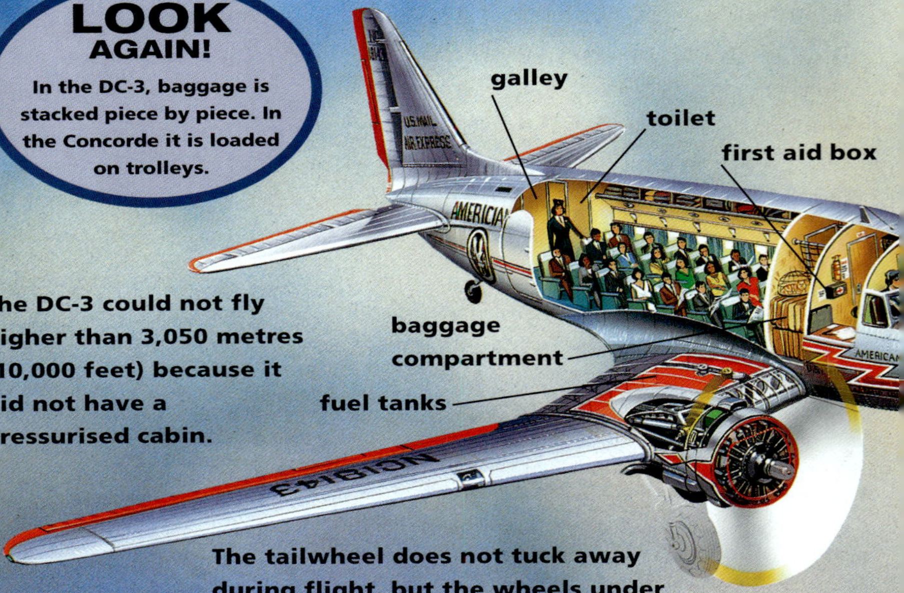

The DC-3 could not fly higher than 3,050 metres (10,000 feet) because it did not have a pressurised cabin.

The tailwheel does not tuck away during flight, but the wheels under the main part of the plane do.

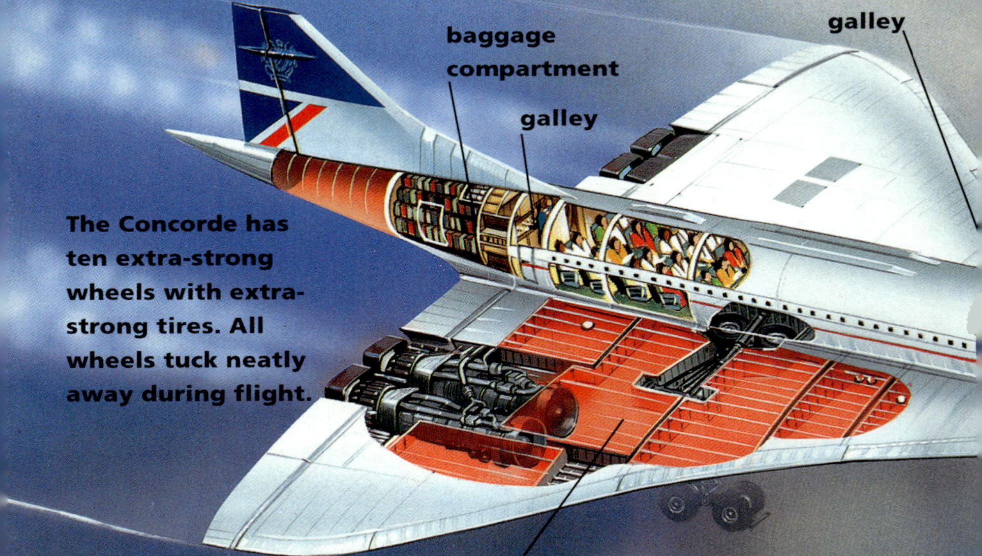

The Concorde has ten extra-strong wheels with extra-strong tires. All wheels tuck neatly away during flight.

The Concorde has four jet engines.

People movers

Passenger planes are called airliners. Since the first airliners flew in the 1930s, passenger aircraft have become larger and faster and can fly non-stop for much longer distances.

A NEW WORLD OF TRAVEL

Travelling in the first passenger planes was a bit like being in a flying railway carriage. The DC-3 first entered service with American Airlines in 1936. It carried 21 passengers in seats like armchairs. There was a kitchen (on planes, a kitchen is called a galley) where food was freshly cooked and in some DC-3s there were even sleeping berths. Today, Boeing 747s, called jumbo jets, can carry 400 passengers—that's 36 World Cup Soccer teams. Passengers eat food that was prepared in giant kitchens on the ground, then chilled and loaded onto the plane in trolleys to be reheated when needed.

When flying, the nose of the plane is raised so the Concorde is totally streamlined. The nose is lowered when landing so the pilot can see more.

LOOK AGAIN!

The pump between the crop duster's wheels sends chemicals to nozzles under the wings.

Crop dusters can quickly spray large areas with pesticide.

ON THE JOB

Farmers use small planes to check on their herds and to round up cattle and horses. They can also spray pesticide from the air. Small planes drop supplies to people cut off by flood or suffering from famine, and they carry cargo and mail into isolated or rugged country, like the mountains of Central America. In Australia, the Royal Flying Doctor Service uses planes to bring medical services to people in remote areas. Small planes protect swimmers by searching for sharks near beaches. They are also used for sightseeing and pleasure flights. Small planes do not need long runways. Some can land on beaches, roads and fields.

At work and play

Small planes can make many jobs faster and easier. They can also reach places that would take too long or are not possible to reach by road, or where larger planes can't land.

A float plane can land only on water. The wheels are at the front so that the plane can be picked up at the back and pushed like a wheelbarrow on land.

SEAPLANES

Seaplanes with hulls like boats are also called flying boats. In the 1930s, before the development of airliners, flying boats were the only aircraft to carry passengers across great stretches of water like the Atlantic and Pacific Oceans. Planes that have floats instead of landing wheels are called float planes. The floats usually have small rudders on the back so the pilot can steer the plane when it is in the water. Flying boats with a single hull, or float planes with a single float, need side floats or wingtip floats to keep them upright when they are landing and taking off.

LOOK AGAIN!

See the hull of the water bomber? This tells us that the aircraft is actually a flying boat.

DASHING

Some water bombers don't need to land at an airstrip to refill their water tanks. They can simply scoop water from any nearby lake, river or the sea. The pilot first swoops low over the surface to check that there is no floating debris that could damage the aircraft. Then the plane sweeps around and down and flies along just touching the water. It takes about ten seconds to scoop up a full load of water.

Water bomber

Some aircraft can be used to dump water on fires burning in places that are difficult to reach by road.

SPLASHING

The Canadair CL-215 Water Bomber was the first aircraft specially designed to fight fires. Built into its strong body are water tanks that can hold up to 5,345 litres (1,175 gallons), about as much as 35 full bath tubs. In the bottom of the tanks are outward-opening doors. Sometimes firefighting foam is added to the water. Foam acts like a blanket over the fire, and reduces smoke, making it safer for firefighting aircraft. Foam is also easy to see when the pilot is working out where to drop the next load.

With all tank doors open, the CL-215 can drop all its water in one second.

Jumping out of a plane

Air filling a parachute slows down a weight falling from the sky. Parachutes are used for escaping from a damaged aircraft, to drop troops, equipment and supplies, and in the sport of sky diving.

LANDING SAFELY

The first parachutes were made of canvas. Later silk was used, and today they are made of nylon. The part of the parachute that fills with air is called the canopy. The first parachutes had round canopies, like umbrellas. Today most parachutes have a rectangular shape. The canopy is made up of many panels, and each panel has many smaller sections, so if there is a tear, the parachutist will not be in danger. Parachutes are important in war. They can be used to drop soldiers, called paratroopers, and spies into enemy territory. In peacetime they are used to drop food and medicine to places where a plane cannot land. In an emergency, a pilot can parachute out of a damaged aircraft. In supersonic planes, parachutes are built into the pilot's ejection seat.

After automatically pulling the canopy open, the nylon cord breaks, and the parachutist floats to the ground.

LOOK AGAIN!

The pilot switches the light near the door to green when the aircraft is over the jump zone.

The parachutist swings clear of the aircraft, but is still connected to the plane by a strap and a nylon cord. These are attached to the line which automatically opens the chute.

The parachute is packed in a strong nylon container and attached to the parachutist's body by a harness that fits around the body and legs.

Spy in the sky

Gathering information about an area is called reconnaissance or spying. Reconnaissance planes photograph and check on enemy sites and troop movements. They try to hide in many different ways. Some fly at night. Some fly fast and low to avoid radar. Some use camouflage.

The Lockheed SR-71 Blackbird. Cameras and other equipment are carried in the nose cone and along the sides of the plane.

The red markings show fragile areas that must not be walked on when maintenance work is being done on the aircraft.

powerful turbojet engine

LOOK AGAIN!

The higher the plane goes, the darker the sky gets. Eventually, in space, it is all black.

HIGH FLIER

The Lockheed SR-71 Blackbird, pictured here, flies at extremely high altitudes. It is also the fastest jet ever, and can reach 3,523 kilometres (2,189 miles) per hour. At this great speed the friction (rubbing) of air against the outer surfaces of its wings causes them to become very hot. The SR-71 is made of a special heat-resistant metal called titanium alloy. Titanium alloy is about as strong as stainless steel, but weighs about half as much. The SR-71 Blackbird can photograph 160,000 square kilometres (100,000 square miles)—an area greater than the entire United Kingdom—in just one hour.

LOOK AGAIN!

The orbiter seems to be flying upside down. This protects the crew from the sun's fierce heat.

The orbiter is covered in more than 24,000 special heat-absorbing tiles to stop it from burning up as it re-enters the Earth's atmosphere.

The space shuttle is put into orbit by powerful engines. These separate from the shuttle after launching.

communications satellite

Crew members wear oxygen-filled space suits and life-support backpacks.

The orbiter's robot arm holds the communications satellite while crew carry out maintenance work.

in space

The space shuttles are reusable aircraft for going into space and coming back. One of their main uses is to transport communication satellites into space.

OUT OF THIS WORLD

The shuttle is blasted into space by its three rocket engines assisted by two recoverable booster rockets that are jettisoned at an altitude of 46 kilometres (28 miles). What is left contains the crew and cargo, and is called the orbiter. On its return journey to Earth, the orbiter is just like a huge glider. The pilot slows it down by doing a number of big bends until it is at the right height and in the right place to land. The first reusable space craft was the NASA Space Shuttle *Columbia*, launched in 1981. Scientists are also working on rocket airliners that would fly partly in the Earth's atmosphere, and partly in space, so the journey from one side of the Earth to the other would take only two or three hours.

White screens shield equipment from the sun's rays while the cargo bay doors are open.

The nose cone and front part of the wings are made of an extremely strong material called reinforced carbon-carbon. It can withstand temperatures of up to 1,650°C (3,000°F).

Keeping a plane in your garage

You'll need a lot of space and a lot of equipment if you want to keep a plane at home. You'll also need very understanding neighbours.

HOW ABOUT A HAWKER HARRIER?

A good choice would be a Hawker Harrier, because it can take off vertically. Most other planes need a runway. However, taking off this way uses up more fuel, so you will have to build fuel storage tanks in the garden. Measure your garage. Although it is a small plane, the Harrier is still 12 metres (46 feet) long, 4 metres (12 feet) high and 10 metres (31 feet) wide. Will it fit in the garage?

Some neighbours may complain about the noise!

Make your own paper plane

1. Fold the corners up along fold 1. Crease down. Repeat for fold 2.

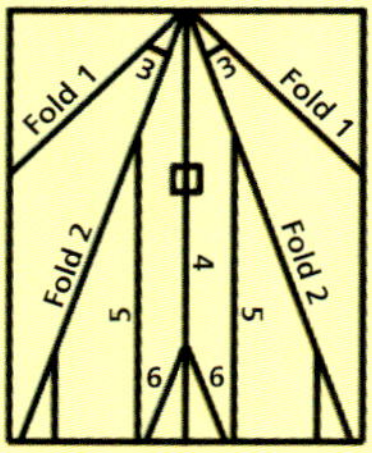

2. Fold the nose back, along fold 3.
3. Fold up along fold 4.
5. Fold down each wing at fold 5.
   Turn down the wing tips along fold 6.
6. Your plane is now ready to decorate.
   Throw angled slightly up. How far can it fly?

GLOSSARY

aerofoil The curved and dynamic shape of a wing or propeller blade.

air pressure The weight of the air that pushes down on all objects.

altitude The height above the ground or above sea level.

battle group An aircraft carrier and its destroyers or cruise escorts.

biplane An aircraft with two sets of wings, one above the other.

cockpit The compartment at the front of the aircraft containing all the controls, and in which the pilot sits.

dogfight A battle at close range between two or more fighter planes.

drag The force of the air that acts on a plane in the opposite direction to thrust.

ejection seat An explosive charge that fires a pilot or crew member's seat out of a disabled jet aircraft, taking it clear of the tail plane. The seat falls away as the parachute opens.

exhaust The outlet parts of an engine through which waste gases escape.

force Push or pull acting upon objects. The four forces that act upon aeroplanes are gravity, lift, drag and thrust.

formation A group of aircraft flying together.

friction The resistance made when air moves over a plane.

fuselage The body of an aircraft.

galley The kitchen in an airliner.

glider An aircraft that usually does not have an engine and needs rising air for lift.

gravity The force that pulls objects towards the earth. Planes must overcome the force of gravity in order to fly.

landing gear The wheels that support an aircraft on the ground.

lift The force that acts against the pull of gravity and raises objects upwards.

GLOSSARY

low observable aircraft Aircraft that are invisible or nearly so to usual radar or infra-red detection.

Luftwaffe The German Airforce.

manoeuvres (man–oo–vers) The planned movements of an aircraft in flight. Fighter pilots in World War I and World War II needed skill to perform manoeuvres in the air.

monoplane An aircraft with one set of wings.

orbit To move in a curved path around the Earth or another planet.

pitch The tilting of an aircraft up or down.

radar (Radio Detecting And Ranging) A method of detecting aircraft using radio waves, which bounce back off the aircraft and signal its position on the radar screen.

range The safe distance an aircraft can travel without running out of fuel.

roll (bank) The movement of a plane from side to side.

rotor A blade that provides lift for a helicopter or autogyro.

thrust The force that pushes an aircraft forwards through the air.

triplane An aircraft with three sets of wings, one above the other.

turbine A large-bladed fan in a jet engine, which is turned by the movement of air.

turbojet Jet engines propelled forward by gaseous fluid.

stealth technology Stealth technology makes aircraft or satellites invisible or nearly so to usual radar or infra-red detection.

supersonic Moving or capable of moving faster than the speed of sound.

yaw The turning movement of a plane to left or right.

FIND OUT MORE ABOUT PLANES

BOOKS

Greenwood, John (ed), *Milestones of Aviation,* Smithsonian Institute, National Air and Space Museum, Washington, 1989.

Haslam, Andrew, *Make it Work! Flight,* Reader's Digest, Sydney, 1995.

Johnstone, Michael and Jenssen, Hans, *Look Inside Cross-Sections*: Planes, Dorling Kindersley, London, 1994.

Marriott, Leo, *Eighty Years of Civil Aviation,* Promotional Reprint Company, London, 1997.

Mondey, David (ed), *The Illustrated Encyclopedia of World Aircraft,* Golden Press, Sydney, 1978.

Ogilvy, David, Shuttleworth. *The Historic Aeroplanes,* Airlife Publishing, Shrewsbury, 1989.

WEBSITES

Australian Aviation Museum
http://www.bankstownairport. com.au

Boeing
http://www.boeing.com

NASA Public Affairs Office
pao@dfrc.nasa.gov

Royal Air Force
http://www.raf.mod.uk

Santa Monica Museum of Flying
http://www.mof.org/mof

Smithsonian Institute (Air and Space)
http://www.airspacemag.Earthlink.net

Weeks Air Museum, Florida
http://www.weeksairmuseum.com

INDEX

INDEX

FREE

POSTER!

Collect 6 of the gold INVESTIGATE stickers

(you will find one on the stickers' page in each book).

Send all 6 stickers on a sheet of paper along with your name and address to:

Investigate Series Poster
Whitecap Books
351 Lynn Avenue
North Vancouver
British Columbia
V7J 2C4

and we'll send you your free INVESTIGATE series poster.

Please allow 21 days for delivery.